ALL ABOUT

ANCIENT EGYPT

Published by Collins
An imprint of HarperCollins*Publishers*
1 Robroyston Gate, Glasgow, G33 1JN

HarperCollins*Publishers*
Macken House, 39/40 Mayor Street Upper, Dublin 1, D01 C9W8, Ireland

collins.co.uk

First published 2026

© HarperCollins*Publishers* 2026

Collins® is a registered trademark of HarperCollins*Publishers* Ltd.

Text by: Sonya Newland
'Ask an expert' contribution by: Aliaa Ismail

Publisher: Michelle I'Anson
Project leader: Rachel Allegro
Cover and interior design: James Hunter & Rachel Allegro
Editorial: Tracey Cowell & Louise Robb
Production: Ilaria Rovera

Photo credits
All photos © Shutterstock, except: p.12(b): Art Collection 3 / Alamy; p.17(c): Science History Images / Alamy; p.20(c): GRANGER – Historical Picture Archive / Alamy; p.26(b): Lanmas / Alamy; p.27(b): Penta Springs Limited / Alamy; p.31(Nut): Ivy Close Images / Alamy; p.31(Osiris): Lanmas / Alamy; p.32(c): Heritage Image Partnership Ltd / Alamy; p.35(t): The Print Collector / Alamy; p.36: Lanmas / Alamy; p.37(c): Magica / Alamy; p.47(b): World History Archive / Alamy; p.49(b): CPA Media Pte Ltd / Alamy; p.52(Djed): World History Archive / Alamy; p.59(b): Art Directors & TRIP / Alamy; p.62(t): Peter Horree / Alamy; p.63(t): Archive PL / Alamy; p.63(b): Alain Guilleux / Alamy; p.64(t): Michael Ventura / Alamy; p.64(b): Balint Takacs; p.66(c): Science History Images / Alamy; p.68(b): Papilio / Alamy; p.72(b): GRANGER – Historical Picture Archive / Alamy; p.73(b): The Picture Art Collection / Alamy; p.76(t): Aliaa Ismail; p76-77: Aliaa Ismail; p.78(t): Lanmas; p.81(t): IanDagnall Computing / Alamy; p.81(b): Realy Easy Star / Alamy; p.83(t): The Print Collector / Alamy; p.83(b): Colin Waters / Alamy; p.84(no.2): Historic Images / Alamy; p.84(no.3): MET/BOT / Alamy; p.84(no.5): World History Archive / Alamy; p.84(no.6): ART Collection / Alamy; p.85(no.14): WBC ART / Alamy

The contents of this publication are believed correct at the time of printing. Every care has been taken in the preparation of this book. However, the publisher can accept no responsiblity for errors or omissions, changes in detail given or for any expense or loss thereby caused.

A catalogue record for this book is available from the British Library.

ISBN 9780008776176

Printed in India by Replika Press Pvt. Ltd.

10 9 8 7 6 5 4 3 2 1

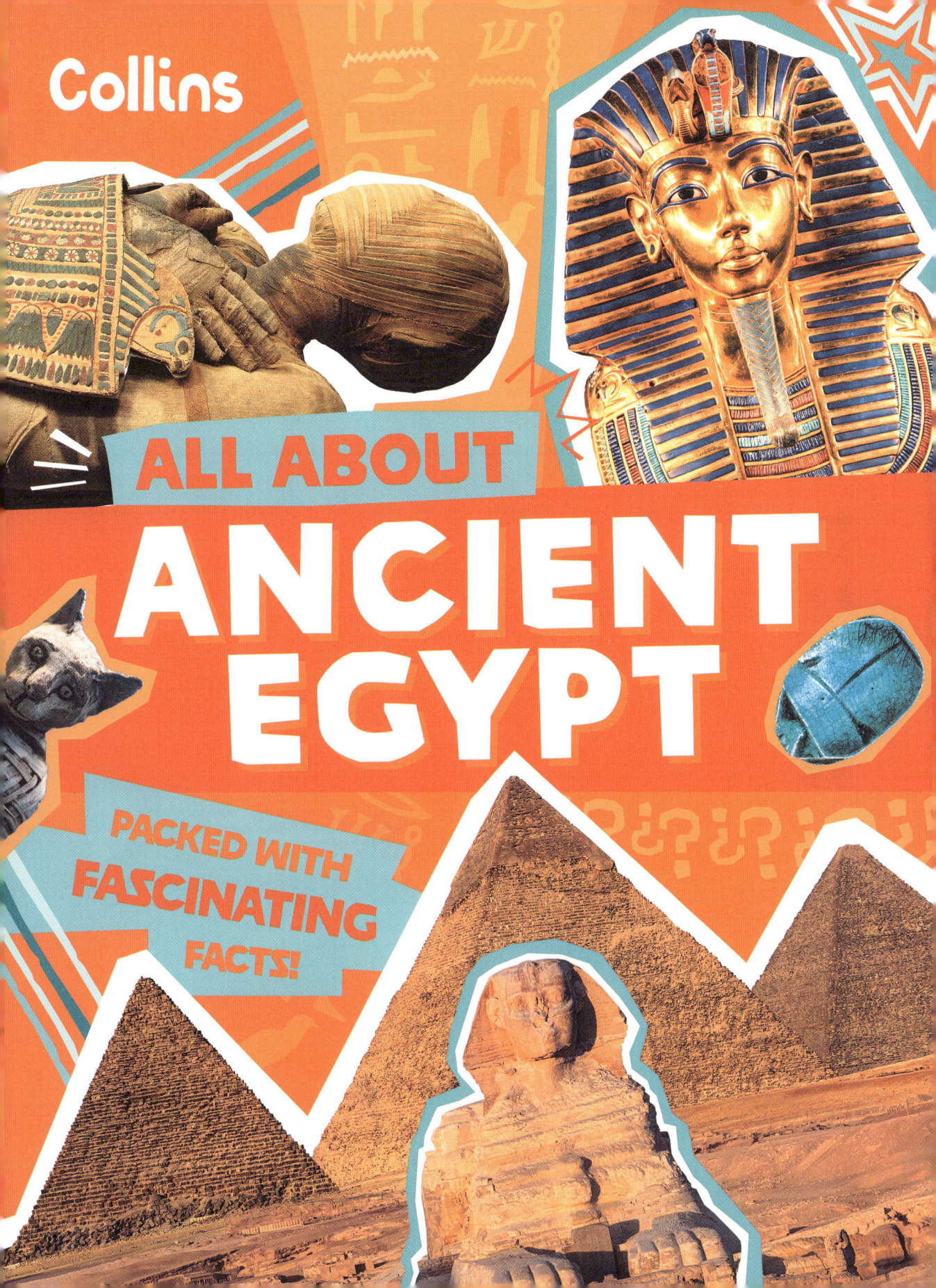

Collins

ALL ABOUT

ANCIENT EGYPT

PACKED WITH
FASCINATING
FACTS!

CONTENTS

The Egyptian civilisation

Ancient Egypt was a powerful civilisation that grew up along the River Nile in northern Africa. It lasted for more than 3,000 years, and is remembered today for its pharaohs, gods and goddesses, art and architecture, as well as some amazing inventions.

ANCIENT HISTORY

Human ancestors evolved an incredible 6 million years ago, but modern humans, *Homo sapiens*, are much younger – only about 300,000 years old. Early humans lived in small, isolated groups. However, over thousands of years larger societies formed, and out of these grew some mighty civilisations.

What makes a civilisation?

Ancient civilisations were more than just groups of people. They were advanced societies with cities, systems of government, social structures and religious beliefs. These ancient people had ways of writing and record-keeping, and they established laws to help everyone live together. They traded goods with each other and formed armies to protect their lands.

'c.' is short for 'circa', a Latin word meaning 'around' or 'about'. So c. in this timeline means around that time, as we don't know the dates for certain.

Major moments

C. 3500-539 BCE
Mesopotamia (modern Iraq and north-east Syria)

C. 3100-30 BCE
Ancient Egypt (modern Egypt)

C. 2100 BCE -CE 220
Ancient China (modern China)

C. 3300-1300 BCE
Indus Valley Civilisation (modern Pakistan and north-west India)

C. 2600-1400 BCE
Minoan Civilisation (modern Greek islands)

The first civilisations

No one can say for sure which was the first great civilisation. Probably several powerful societies developed at about the same time, somewhere between 5,000 and 6,000 years ago. They grew up around rivers, because people could settle in one place there and make a living by farming. You can see some of the most famous ancient civilisations on the timeline below.

A lasting impact

The impact of ancient civilisations echoes through time to the present day. During this period of history, people invented writing, mathematics, laws and calendars. They built extraordinary monuments and created art and literature that inspires people even today. Experts still study ancient civilisations to learn how people lived in the past and how human society has changed over time.

C. 1600-1100 BCE
Mycenaean Civilisation (modern mainland Greece)

C. 559-331 BCE
Persian Empire (modern Iran, Egypt and Türkiye)

C. 2000 BCE -CE 1600
Maya Civilisation (modern southern Mexico and Central America)

C. 753 BCE -CE 476
Ancient Rome (modern Italy)

C. 510-323 BCE
Classical Greece (modern Greece)

THE RISE & FALL OF ANCIENT EGYPT

The civilisation of Ancient Egypt lasted a very long time – around 3,000 years. Throughout its history, the civilisation's fortunes rose and fell several times. There were periods of peace and stability. There were also times of invasion, unrest and famine.

Early Egypt

People began to live in Egypt more than 8,000 years ago. As time passed, these small settlements of hunters and fishermen merged to become villages and then states. Eventually there were two large kingdoms – Lower Egypt and Upper Egypt. In around 3100 BCE, these united to form one potentially powerful civilisation.

FASCINATING FACT

The River Nile flows from south to north, so the Ancient Egyptians considered the southern part of the region to be 'up'. That's why Lower Egypt was the northern kingdom and Upper Egypt was the southern one.

The Three Kingdoms

The history of Ancient Egypt is broadly divided into three 'kingdoms'. These weren't geographical areas, but periods of time: the Old Kingdom (2686–2181 BCE), the Middle Kingdom (2055–1650 BCE) and the New Kingdom (1550–1070 BCE). During these times, Egypt enjoyed peace and prosperity.

Tuthmose II was a pharaoh of the New Kingdom.

Intermediate periods

In between the years of the Three Kingdoms were 'intermediate periods'. During these times, Ancient Egypt suffered under weak leaders. There was political instability, and life was hard for the Egyptian people.

The end of Ancient Egypt

After the New Kingdom, Ancient Egypt began to decline. One after another, foreign powers invaded and controlled the region. In 30 BCE, the Roman leader Octavian conquered Egypt, marking the end of the Ancient Egyptian civilisation.

Octavian became Roman Emperor Augustus in 27 BCE.

WHO WERE THE ANCIENT EGYPTIANS?

At the top of Egyptian society was the pharaoh (the king). Below him were the priests, nobles and officials, followed by soldiers and scribes (see page 27). Merchants and craftsmen held mid-level status. At the bottom were farmers and labourers, and then enslaved people.

Farmers

Most ordinary Egyptians were farmers. They lived near the banks of the River Nile in houses made of mud bricks. They relied on the river's seasonal floods to grow crops such as wheat, barley and flax.

Traders

Traders were an important part of Ancient Egyptian society. They exchanged goods made or grown in Egypt, like papyrus and grain, for wood such as cedar and ebony, animal skins – and even live animals!

TRUE OR FALSE?

Scribes were important because most people in Ancient Egypt couldn't read or write.

Find out on p.88!

Soldiers

Ancient Egypt had a well-organised and highly disciplined army. They were mostly foot soldiers, armed with spears and shields. Some soldiers rode chariots and fought with bows and arrows.

Enslaved people

Many enslaved people were foreigners who had been captured in war, but there were other types of enslavement, too. People who had debts could volunteer to be enslaved to pay them off. The state sometimes forced Egyptian citizens (usually peasants) to work as labourers on big projects like building canals and temples, in return for food and clothing. This often happened during the annual Nile flood, when peasants couldn't work the land.

THE RIVER NILE

The Nile was the heart of life in Ancient Egypt. It provided water, food, transport and fertile land for farming. Without it, the Egyptian civilisation would never have existed.

Floods and farming

Egypt is a desert country – hot and dry – but the River Nile made it possible for people to farm there. Every year, the river flooded the surrounding land, leaving behind a rich, black soil that was perfect for growing crops.

Trade and transport

The river provided a convenient way of getting around. Boats carried people and goods between towns and cities along the banks of the Nile. It also allowed the Ancient Egyptians to trade with other cultures in Africa and the Mediterranean.

Boats on the Nile

The simplest boats were called skiffs, which were made of papyrus reeds tied together with rope. These were used mainly for travelling short distances or for reaching a good fishing spot. The Ancient Egyptians also built bigger boats out of wood, with a big sail in the middle to speed them along.

ZOOM IN

The Egyptians used heavy acacia wood for the bottom of their boats, so they would be strong enough to carry heavy loads.

Hapi was the Ancient Egyptian god of the annual Nile flood.

A spiritual place

The Ancient Egyptians believed that the Nile was a gift from the gods. The annual flood was so important that it had its own god – Hapi. Other gods were linked to the Nile, too, and the river featured in the myths, rituals and daily prayers of the Egyptian people.

FASCINATING FACT

Each year, Egyptians have a two-week holiday in August called Wafaa El-Nil to celebrate the ancient flooding of the Nile. These days, though, the Nile no longer floods. In 1970, the Aswan High Dam was built to control the flow of the river all year round, in order to provide drinking water and water for farms, and to generate electricity.

FAMOUS PLACES

Great cities grew up along the Nile. The remains of some of these important centres can still be seen. Others we only know about because of records left by the Ancient Egyptians – no evidence of them has been found ... yet!

Thebes

Ancient Egypt's capital city changed several times, but Thebes held the title for hundreds of years. Known as 'Waset' to the Ancient Egyptians, the main city lay on the east bank of the Nile. It was home to important temples like Luxor and Karnak.

The City of the Dead

On the opposite bank of the Nile, the other part of Thebes was the necropolis – the 'City of the Dead', where important people were buried. The famous Valley of the Kings and Valley of the Queens were part of this burial complex.

Memphis

Memphis was the capital of ancient Egypt for around 800 years, during the Old Kingdom, and it may once have been the biggest city in the world. It was an important centre of trade and religion. It even had its own god – Ptah, a god of arts, crafts and architects. The remains of the huge temple to Ptah still stand today.

Alexandria

Alexandria was founded after Alexander the Great conquered Egypt, in 331 BCE. It was Egypt's capital for nearly 1,000 years. It was a great centre of culture and learning, home to a famous library, and the Lighthouse of Alexandria – one of the Seven Wonders of the Ancient World.

 5 lost cities of ancient Egypt

1. Thinis – the first capital city of Upper Egypt

2. Naukratis – an ancient port city in the Nile Delta

3. Heracleion – a city swallowed up by the Mediterranean Sea

4. The Dazzling City of Aten – a city dedicated to the sun god, Aten, which was only discovered in 2020

5. Itjtawy – the exact location of this former capital city has not yet been found

LAND & PEOPLE

Here are some fascinating facts and figures about the people of Ancient Egypt and the land that they called home.

Longest river

The Nile is often considered to be the longest river in the world. It stretches nearly 6,700 kilometres through 11 countries.

Population explosion

At the start of the Ancient Egyptian civilisation, the population of the region was somewhere between 1 and 1.5 million. At its height it may have been more than 3 million.

River life

Over 90 per cent of all the people in Ancient Egypt lived in the Nile's floodplain – the area along its banks that flooded every year.

Country of capitals

Throughout its 3,000-year history, more than 10 different cities served as the capital of Ancient Egypt.

Nome numbers

Ancient Egypt was typically divided into 42 administrative regions, called nomes. There were 22 nomes in Upper Egypt and 20 in Lower Egypt.

Pyramid builders

More than 130 pyramids have been discovered all over Egypt. The Great Pyramid at Giza (see page 39) took tens of thousands of workers more than 20 years to build.

Tomb-tastic

The Valley of the Kings was the burial ground for Egyptian pharaohs for over 500 years. More than 60 tombs have been found there.

A modern queen

Cleopatra (see page 23) – the last pharaoh of Egypt – lived closer to you in time (just over 2,000 years ago) than to the building of the pyramids at Giza (about 2,500 years before she lived).

Kings and dynasties

Egypt was ruled by around 170 pharaohs. They are grouped into 31 ruling families, or dynasties.

WHO WERE THE PHARAOHS?

For long periods of its history, Ancient Egypt was ruled by a series of kings who belonged to particular dynasties, or royal families. These kings were known as pharaohs (pronounced 'fair-ohs'). The word pharaoh means 'Great House', which refers to the palace where the king lived.

Head of state

The pharaoh had absolute power over all the land and people in Egypt. He was the royal ruler and head of state, in charge of the government. He was also commander of the armies of Egypt, and was expected to lead his soldiers into battle if a foreign power threatened his kingdom.

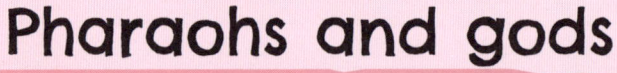
Tutankhamun leading his army.

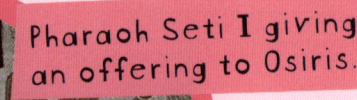
Pharaoh Seti 1 giving an offering to Osiris.

Pharaohs and gods

Pharaohs were also religious leaders. The Egyptian people believed that the pharaoh was divine – a link between their world and the world of the gods – and it was the pharaoh's job to make sure the gods were happy. While a pharaoh was alive, he was associated with the god Horus. After he died, he was associated with a different god, Osiris – the ruler of the underworld.

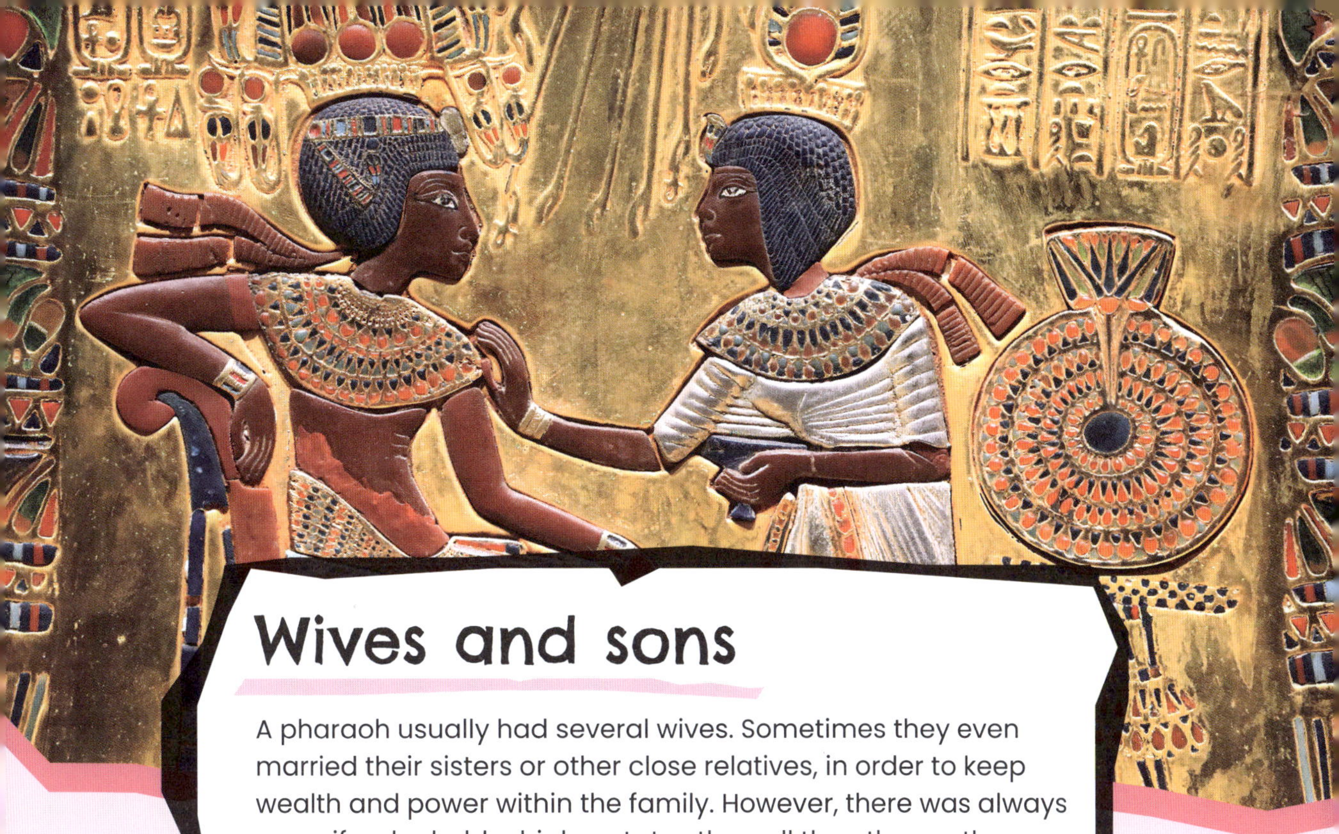

Wives and sons

A pharaoh usually had several wives. Sometimes they even married their sisters or other close relatives, in order to keep wealth and power within the family. However, there was always one wife who held a higher status than all the others – the 'Great Royal Wife'. When a pharaoh died, the eldest son of his Great Royal Wife usually inherited the throne.

5 famous pharaohs

1. Narmer (ruled c. 3100 BCE): United Upper and Lower Egypt to become the first ruler of a unified kingdom; also known as Menes.

2. Djoser (ruled 2686–2649 BCE): Built the Step Pyramid, Egypt's first large-scale stone monument.

3. Thutmose III (ruled 1458–1425 BCE): A warrior king who expanded Egypt's empire and who may have been the greatest pharaoh ever.

4. Tutankhamun (ruled 1332–1323 BCE): A boy king famous because of the discovery of his tomb filled with amazing artefacts (objects made by humans), including a beautiful golden death mask.

5. Seti I (ruled 1290–1279 BCE): A skilled military leader who built grand temples and restored Egypt's reputation.

QUEENS OF EGYPT

Women did not often become pharaohs, but a few did. Being the wife or mother of a pharaoh was also an important and respected job, and the queen symbolised the power of birth and creation.

Sobekneferu (ruled 1763–1760 BCE)

Historians think that Sobekneferu was the first woman to rule in her own right. She was the daughter of Pharaoh Amenemhat III, but there were no men in the family to take the throne after Sobekneferu's half-brother died, so she took the title herself.

Hatshepsut (ruled 1478–1458 BCE)

Hatshepsut ruled with her young stepson, Thutmose III, for some of the time, but she might also have been pharaoh in her own right for a few years. One of her biggest successes as leader was sponsoring an important trading expedition to a place called Punt. The explorers brought back great wealth in the form of gold and ebony. Hatshepsut also built magnificent temples and two huge obelisks at Karnak.

Queen Hatshepsut's famous trading expedition

Nefertiti
(ruled 1353–1336 BCE)

The powerful and beautiful Nefertiti was Great Royal Wife to Amenhotep IV (later called Akhenaten), and may have ruled equally with him. Nefertiti helped her husband lead a religious revolution in Egypt, when they decided to worship only one god – the Aten – instead of many.

Cleopatra VII
(ruled 51–30 BCE)

Cleopatra was a member of the Ptolemy dynasty, which had been ruling the kingdom for nearly 300 years. She was a brilliant leader and a clever politician, and went to war with her own brother so that she could win the crown. On her death in 30 BCE, Egypt fell to the Romans, so Cleopatra is considered the last pharaoh of Ancient Egypt.

TRUE OR FALSE?

Cleopatra had a child with the famous Roman ruler, Julius Caesar.

Find out on p.88!

RAMESES THE GREAT

Rameses II is one of the most famous pharaohs in the history of Egypt. His 66-year reign was a golden age of peace and prosperity in the kingdom, and he is remembered as 'Rameses the Great'.

A soldier king

Rameses was a great warrior who led the Egyptian army into many battles. One of the most famous was a huge chariot battle at Kadesh, fought against the Hittites – a group of people who came from the area that is now Türkiye. There was no clear winner, but Rameses claimed victory and filled temples with carvings showing his heroism.

Major moments

C. 1303 BCE
Rameses is born to Pharaoh Seti I and Queen Tuya.

1279 BCE
Rameses becomes pharaoh at the age of about 25.

C. 1288 BCE
Rameses marries Nefertari while they are both still teenagers.

1275 BCE
Rameses's capital, Pi-Rameses, is at its height as a centre for the military and industry in Egypt.

Master builder

Throughout his long life, Rameses oversaw hundreds of building projects. He built great temples to worship the gods, and statues to emphasise his own power. He even built a new capital city, called Pi-Rameses. His most famous construction is a vast temple carved into a mountainside at Abu Simbel. It was guarded by four colossal statues of Rameses himself.

A family man

Rameses II had lots of wives – and more than 100 children! His favourite queen was Nefertari, and Rameses built temples and statues in her honour, too. The pharaoh gave his sons important jobs so they stayed loyal to him, and this helped keep the kingdom peaceful and strong. Rameses lived longer than his 12 oldest sons, so when he died, his 13th son Merneptah became pharaoh.

Queen Nefertari

1274 BCE
Rameses fights the Hittites in the Battle of Kadesh – the first known battle that recorded military tactics in detail.

1258 BCE
The first-ever peace treaty is signed, between Rameses and Hittite leader Hattusili III.

C. 1264 BCE
The great temple at Abu Simbel started to be built.

1213 BCE
Rameses II dies at the age of around 90.

THE VIZIER, PRIESTS & SCRIBES

Although the pharaoh had absolute power, he relied on different groups of people to help him govern his land and people effectively.

The vizier

The pharaoh's most trusted advisor was the vizier – the most powerful man in the country after the pharaoh. The vizier was the chief judge, in charge of making sure that laws were followed. Among his many other duties, he was also the head of the treasury and was responsible for collecting taxes.

Mereruka was vizier to Pharaoh Teti.

Priests

Priests worked in the temples. Their main job was to care for the god or goddess in their particular temple. They would also maintain the whole temple complex and help prepare for festivals and other ceremonies. The pharaoh was considered the high priest of Egypt, but he chose other high priests to share his responsibilities.

Scribes

If you wanted to reach a high status in Ancient Egyptian society, you could also become a scribe. Scribes were responsible for writing everything down, and they were highly respected because they could read and write. They recorded laws, religious texts, trades that were made and taxes that were paid. All of this kept the government, the temples and the Egyptian economy running smoothly. It's thanks to the scribes that we know so much about Ancient Egypt!

FAMOUS FIGURE

Imhotep

Imhotep was a skilled architect, famous for designing Egypt's first pyramid, the Step Pyramid at Saqqara, for Pharaoh Djoser. But Imhotep was also the pharaoh's vizier, and became known for his great wisdom. He was high priest of the sun god Ra in the city of Heliopolis, and was later worshipped as a god of medicine and knowledge himself.

PART ONE

See what you've learned so far by trying to answer these questions on the first part of the book. There are questions on everything from the rise and fall of Ancient Egypt to its geography, people and pharaohs... Good luck!

Check your answers on p.89!

1 When did *Homo sapiens* evolve?

A. 6 million years ago

B. 300,000 years ago

C. 10,000 years ago

2 What happened in 3100 BCE?

A. Lower Egypt and Upper Egypt were united

B. The Great Pyramid of Giza was built

C. Egypt was taken over by the Romans

3 How many 'kingdoms' of Ancient Egypt were there?

A. Two

B. Three

C. Four

4 What job did most ordinary Egyptians do?

A. They were soldiers.

B. They were scribes.

C. They were farmers.

TRUE OR FALSE?

Rameses II had the shortest reign of any Egyptian pharaoh.

Find out on p.88!

5 Which city did the Ancient Egyptians call Waset?

A. Thebes

B. Heliopolis

C. Alexandria

6 What 'Wonder of the Ancient World' stood at Alexandria?

A. A pyramid

B. A temple

C. A lighthouse

7 What was a 'nome' in Ancient Egypt??

A. A type of tomb

B. An administrative region

C. A form of money

8 What does the word 'pharaoh' mean?

A. 'Great House'

B. 'Royal King'

C. 'God on Earth'

9 Who was Egypt's last pharaoh?

A. Rameses II

B. Tutankhamun

C. Cleopatra

10 What was the second most powerful position in Ancient Egypt?

A. High priest

B. Vizier

C. Architect

GODS & GODDESSES

The Ancient Egyptians worshipped hundreds of different gods and goddesses (deities).

Ra

God of: The sun

About: Ra had the body of a human and the head of a falcon, with the sun disc wrapped in a cobra (snake) on his head.

Key belief: Ra sailed across the sky in a boat each day and travelled through the underworld at night.

Isis

Goddess of: Magic, healing, motherhood and protection

About: Isis is shown as a woman with a throne-shaped crown, or sometimes with cow horns enclosing a sun disc.

Key belief: Isis used powerful magic to protect her family, especially her son Horus. She helped to bring Osiris back to life after he was murdered.

FASCINATING FACT

Ma'at is the idea of balance and harmony. The Ancient Egyptians performed rituals and offerings so that the gods kept this balance.

Osiris

God of: The afterlife, the dead, resurrection and new life

About: Osiris is shown as a mummified body, with green skin to represent rebirth, and a pharaoh's beard. He is sometimes shown with a headdress that has two ostrich feathers (an atef crown).

Key belief: Osiris was murdered by his brother Seth, and his body was scattered throughout Egypt. He was brought back to life by Isis, and was considered to be the first mummy.

Horus

God of: The sky

About: Horus is depicted with the body of a man and the head of a falcon, or just as a falcon. He is often shown wearing the double crown of Upper and Lower Egypt.

Key belief: Horus was the son of Isis and Osiris. He defeated his uncle Seth to become king. Pharaohs were believed to be living versions of Horus on Earth.

Nut

Goddess of: The sky and the heavens

About: Nut is shown as a woman arching over Earth, often covered in stars.

Key belief: Nut swallowed the sun every night and gave birth to it every morning. She protected and watched over the souls of the dead; they would travel through her body on their way to the afterlife, like the sun did every night.

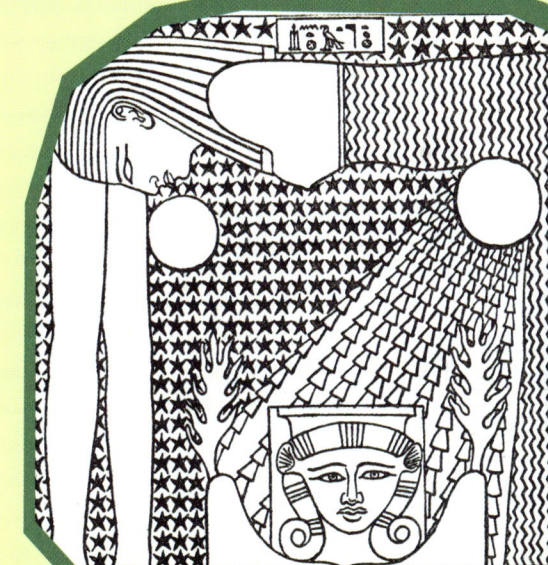

Seth

God of: The desert, storms and chaos

About: Seth is shown in different forms, with the head of a mixture of animals including an aardvark, a donkey and a jackal.

Key belief: Seth was both a hero and a villain. He killed his brother Osiris because he was jealous of him, but he also protected the sun god, Ra.

31

SACRED CATS

The Ancient Egyptians respected and admired many different animals, but the most sacred of all was the cat. Cats were associated with religion, but they also played an important part in everyday life.

Protective powers

Cats were thought to have magical powers. Ancient Egyptians kept them as pets because they believed they could protect the home from evil spirits and disease. In practical terms, cats were natural hunters, so they could also protect the home from pests like rats, mice and snakes!

FASCINATING FACT

Pharaohs often kept big cats such as leopards, cheetahs and especially lions, as a sign of their royal power.

The royal treatment

The Ancient Egyptians treated their cats like royalty. They gave them the best food, and sometimes even dressed them in jewellery! Mummified cats have been found in people's tombs all over Egypt, showing how important they were as much-loved pets and religious offerings to Bastet, the cat goddess. Harming a cat, even by accident, was a serious crime that could be punished by death.

Bastet

Bastet – the cat goddess

The Egyptians worshipped several cat-like goddesses, but the best-loved was Bastet, who had the power to become a cat herself. In paintings she is shown with a human body and a cat's head. A great temple to Bastet was built in the city of Bubastis, and people travelled from far and wide to worship there.

TRUE OR FALSE?

Ancient Egyptians shaved off their eyebrows as a sign of mourning when their cat died.

Find out on p.88!

JOURNEY TO THE AFTERLIFE

For the Ancient Egyptians, life did not end when you died – they believed in an afterlife. To get there, though, a person had to go on a perilous journey through an underworld realm known as Duat.

The ba, the ka and the akh

The Ancient Egyptians believed that everyone was made up of different parts: their physical body, their ka and their ba. The ka was a person's essence, or life force. Even when the body stopped working, you lived on through the ka. The ba was someone's spirit, or personality. After death, these two forces had to reunite to form the akh – the soul that lived on in the afterlife.

The ba is often pictured as a bird with a human head.

TRUE OR FALSE?

The Opening of the Mouth ceremony helped transform a dead person into an akh.

Find out on p.88!

The weighing of the heart

The jackal-headed god Anubis played an important role in the journey through the underworld. He protected the dead and weighed their hearts against the feather of Ma'at – goddess of truth and justice. If the heart was lighter than the feather, that person was allowed to live on in the afterlife.

The Field of Reeds

If the soul passed the test, it was allowed to enter the Field of Reeds – the land of the afterlife, where everything was perfect. It was very much like on Earth, but without any troubles or hardships.

The Book of the Dead

The Book of the Dead was a collection of magical spells and prayers that were often buried with Ancient Egyptians. It was a kind of guide book to the underworld, to help souls pass through safely. The spells protected them from danger on the journey and prepared them for the final judgement.

MAKING MUMMIES

To reach the afterlife, the ba and the ka had to be reunited in a person's body. That's why it was so important to the Ancient Egyptians that they preserved someone's body after they died. They did this through a process called mummification.

Preparing the body

First, priests called embalmers washed the body to make it clean and pure for the afterlife. After that, all the organs were removed and carefully placed in special containers called canopic jars, which were later buried with the person. Usually, only the heart was left in the body.

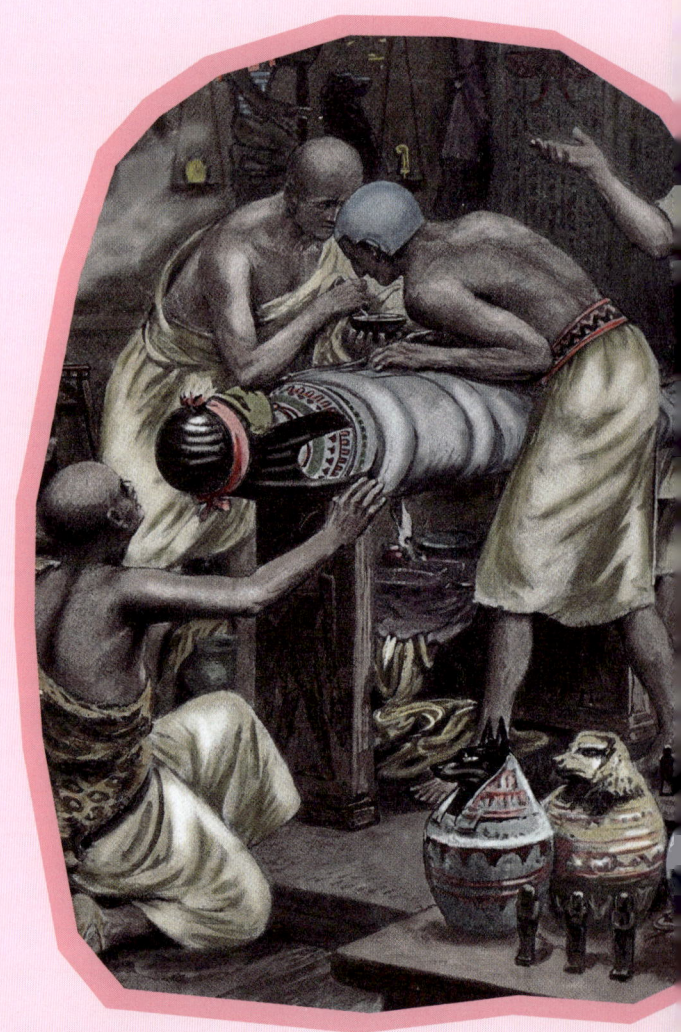

FASCINATING FACT

The brain was not preserved. It was hooked out of the head through the nose and thrown away.

Drying and binding

Next, the body was stuffed and covered in a type of salt called natron. This drew out all the moisture, so the body wouldn't decay. After about 40 days, the salt was removed and the body was cleaned and made to smell nice. The stuffing was also removed. In its place, the embalmers put pieces of cloth or sawdust. They then wound long pieces of cloth like bandages all around the body.

Burying the body

Finally, the body was placed in a coffin called a sarcophagus. This was put in a room inside a tomb, along with all the things that person might need in the afterlife. Items that have been found in Ancient Egyptian tombs include clothes and shoes, jewellery, food, cooking implements and other household items.

FASCINATING FACT

Usually only wealthy people could afford elaborate tombs. Ordinary Egyptians were often simply buried in the desert, where the sand dried and preserved the bodies.

PYRAMIDS

The pyramids have become the most famous symbol of Ancient Egypt. These giant tombs were the final resting place for pharaohs and other important people.

How were the pyramids built?

No one knows exactly how the Ancient Egyptians built such huge structures without modern machinery. Experts think that massive blocks of stone were cut from a quarry and then hauled across the desert on sledges to the building site. There, the blocks were built higher and higher using a system of ramps.

Inside a pyramid

Each pyramid had its own design features. Inside it was a maze of passages and stairways. In addition to the burial chamber, or chambers, there were often store rooms, and even some rooms filled with rocks and rubble to confuse grave robbers if they got in. The walls were covered with paintings that told stories of the person buried there, or with prayers carved into the stone.

Symbols of the sun

The shape of a pyramid represented the sun's rays shining down from the sky. These huge structures were also often positioned so that they lined up with the rising or setting sun on days of the year that were important in Ancient Egyptian religion.

The Great Pyramid of Giza

The biggest pyramid still standing is the Great Pyramid of Giza. It was built for the pharaoh Khufu, who said it would be a stairway for him to reach the afterlife. Completed in 2560 BCE, it was covered in a white stone called limestone, which was polished to a high shine so it glinted like a diamond in the sun.

Top 5 tallest pyramids from Ancient Egypt

1. Great Pyramid of Giza (completed 2560 BCE / 138.5 metres)

2. Pyramid of Khafre (completed 2570 BCE / 136.4 metres)

3. Red Pyramid (2600 BCE / 105 metres)

4. Bent Pyramid (2600 BCE / 104.7 metres)

5. Pyramid of Menkaure (2510 BCE / 65 metres)

TEMPLES

Ancient Egyptian temples were magnificent structures dedicated to particular gods and goddesses, and designed to show off the pharaoh's power. They were believed to be the home of gods and goddesses on Earth, and the pharaoh and high-level priests were allowed into the inner rooms.

Great gateway

One of the first things a visitor to a temple would see was the pylon – a huge stone gateway that surrounded the entrance. The pylon was made up of two massive, sloping towers linked by a doorway. The towers were covered in carvings depicting pharaohs, gods and goddesses, and scenes from important battles. Some pylons had vertical slots or grooves carved in them, where flagpoles would stand.

Inside a temple

The design of a temple interior followed a pattern, leading you from the outside world to sacred rooms. The outer areas might include courtyards that were open to the sunshine. Then there was a large room called the hypostyle hall, with giant columns to hold up the ceiling. Hypostyle is from a Greek term meaning 'under columns'. Smaller rooms eventually led to the most important room of all – the sanctuary. Here, there was a shrine with a statue of the temple's main god or goddess. The inner walls of the temple were covered in carvings and paintings showing the pharaoh in the company of the gods and goddesses.

Rites and rituals

Important rituals were carried out in the temple every day. In the morning, the high priest would go into the sanctuary and greet the statue of the god or goddess. He would wash it and dress it in fine linen, and make offerings of food, incense and rich perfumes. Public festivals were also held in and around the temple. There would be parades of statues of the gods and goddesses, and celebrations in the streets.

FAMOUS FIGURE

Amenhotep, son of Hapu

Amenhotep, son of Hapu, was a brilliant builder and architect in the time of Pharaoh Amenhotep III. He designed the pharaoh's mortuary temple in Thebes. A mortuary temple was somewhere to worship the pharaoh after he died. He also might have helped to build a magnificent temple at Luxor. He was later worshipped as a god of wisdom and healing, and became one of the most honoured non-royal figures in the history of Ancient Egypt.

OBELISKS

Obelisks were tall pillars made of a stone called granite. They had four sides, with a wide base that got narrower the higher up it went, reaching a peak at the top.

Temple guardians

Obelisks were usually placed in pairs on either side of the entrance to the great temples. The Ancient Egyptians associated these monuments with the sun god, Ra, and believed that they connected Earth with the heavens. The pyramid (pyramidion) at the top of an obelisk was covered with gold, or with a precious metal called electrum, so that it reflected the sun's rays.

FASCINATING FACT

The Ancient Romans were fascinated by Egypt. Today, there are more Ancient Egyptian obelisks in the city of Rome – 13 of them – than there are still standing in Egypt.

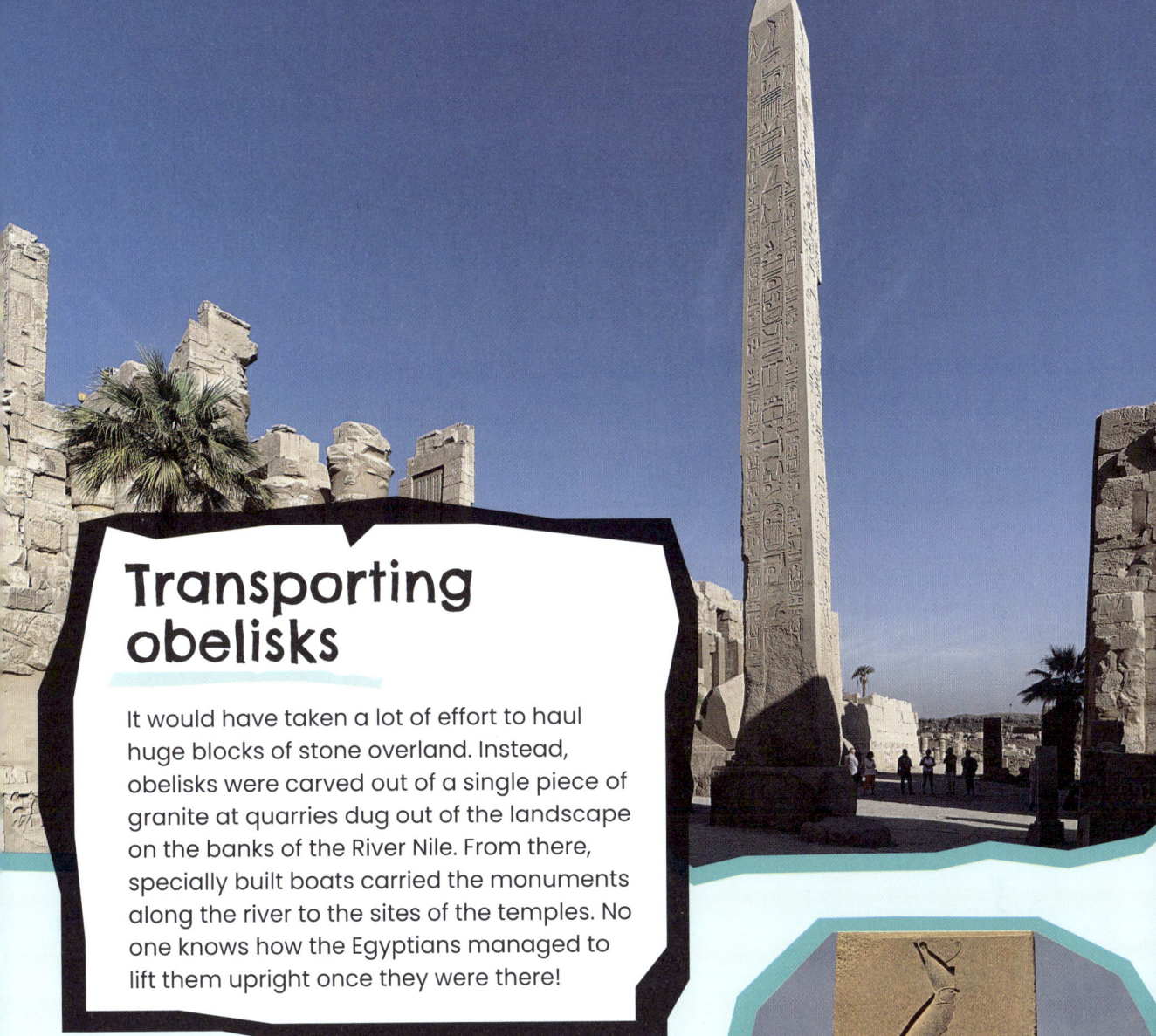

Transporting obelisks

It would have taken a lot of effort to haul huge blocks of stone overland. Instead, obelisks were carved out of a single piece of granite at quarries dug out of the landscape on the banks of the River Nile. From there, specially built boats carried the monuments along the river to the sites of the temples. No one knows how the Egyptians managed to lift them upright once they were there!

Stories in stone

Many obelisks were covered in hieroglyphics (see pages 48-49) that praised not only the gods and goddesses, but also the pharaoh who had them built. These inscriptions told stories of heroic deeds and religious beliefs. The taller the obelisk, the more important the pharaoh appeared to be to the people who saw it.

THE SPHINX

Standing guard over the great pyramids at Giza, in northern Egypt, is one of the most mysterious monuments of Ancient Egypt. The huge statue known as the Great Sphinx of Giza has captured the imagination of writers, poets and historians for hundreds of years.

What is a sphinx?

A sphinx is a mythical creature, usually with the body of a lion and the head of a human (typically a pharaoh). For the Ancient Egyptians, the sphinx was a symbol of the wisdom and strength of the pharaoh and their connection to the gods and goddesses. The 'Avenue of Sphinxes' at Luxor was reopened to the public in 2021. At this time, there were over a thousand statues to see, but more are being uncovered all the time.

The 'Avenue of Sphinxes' at Luxor

The Great Sphinx

The largest sphinx statue in Egypt is one of the biggest sculptures in the whole world. The Great Sphinx of Gaza is 73 metres long and 20 metres high, and was carved about 4,500 years ago. It lies near the pyramids at Giza, and some people think that the sphinx's face might actually be the face of Pharaoh Khufu, or his son Pharaoh Khafre.

ZOOM IN

Pharaoh Thutmose IV had his dream carved into a stele (a stone slab) and put between the front paws of the Great Sphinx.

A dream come true

There are many myths and legends about the Great Sphinx of Giza. One of them tells how a young prince of Egypt fell asleep in its shadow. He had a dream in which the sphinx promised that he would become king if he cleared away the sand that was burying the statue. When he woke up, the prince cleared away the sand. He later became Pharaoh Thutmose IV.

BUILDINGS & BELIEFS

Maths mattered in both religion and architecture in Ancient Egypt! Take a look at these facts and statistics to see how and why.

Numbers of the gods

The Ancient Egyptians worshipped more than 1,400 gods and goddesses. Some experts think there may have been as many as 2,000.

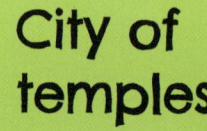

Festival fun

The Festival of Opet, held in Thebes for many centuries, started out at 11 days but grew to become a full 27 days of celebrations.

City of temples

The temple complex at Karnak is one of the largest ever built. This incredible city of temples stretches over an area bigger than 150 football pitches.

Temple supports

In the Great Hypostyle Hall at Karnak, 134 vast columns – some standing at around 21 metres high – are arranged in 16 rows to hold up the temple ceiling.

Building blocks

The Great Pyramid of Giza was constructed from around 2.3 million blocks of stone. Each block weighed between 2.5 and 15 tonnes.

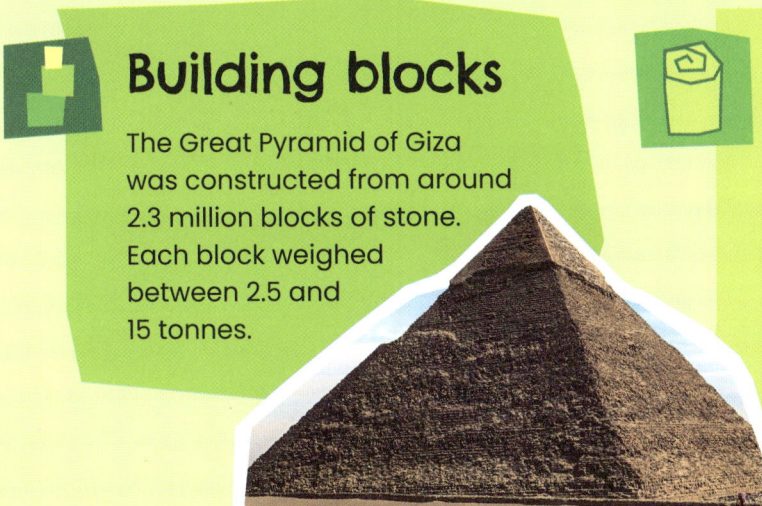

Making a mummy

The process of mummifying a body took about 70 days. Unravelled, the bandages wrapped around the body could stretch up to 1.6 km.

Organ counting

Four canopic jars were used to store a person's organs during mummification. They were represented by the four sons of Horus: Hapi (lungs), Qebehsenuef (intestines), Duamutef (stomach) and Imsety (liver).

Reaching to the sun

Some obelisks weighed over 400 tonnes and stood more than 30 metres tall.

Scroll of spells

Experts think that there were around 200 'chapters' or spells in the Book of the Dead, although it wasn't really a book. It was a collection of spells and text copied onto scrolls.

The Negative Confession

To get into the afterlife, a dead person had to make a 'Negative Confession'. This involved reciting a list of 42 sins that they hadn't committed to 42 minor gods in the underworld.

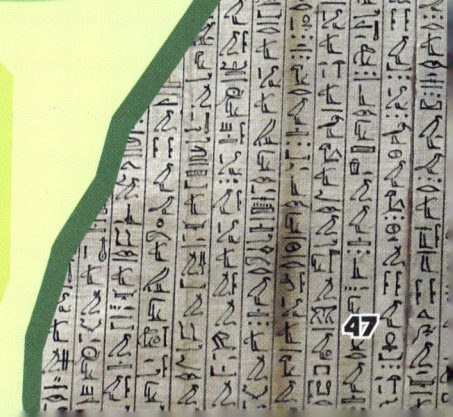

EGYPTIAN WRITING

One of the reasons why we know so much about the Ancient Egyptians is that they left records of many different aspects of their lives. They were one of the first civilisations to develop their spoken language into a written form.

Thoth's words

Thoth was the god of learning and wisdom (and the Moon). The Ancient Egyptians believed that writing was a gift from Thoth, so they referred to their written language as 'medu-netjer', which means 'the god's words'. Today, most people refer to Egyptian writing as 'hieroglyphics', from two Greek words that mean 'sacred carving'.

Writing in pictures

At first, Egyptian writing only used pictures, called pictograms, to represent objects. As writing developed, however, abstract shapes were introduced. These symbols were used to represent more things like names and ideas. Hieroglyphics were designed to look attractive – writing was a form of art in Ancient Egypt.

Understanding hieroglyphics

In the English alphabet, the symbols (letters) represent sounds. But in hieroglyphics, the symbols (hieroglyphs) might represent sounds (phonograms), syllables or even whole words (ideograms). Hieroglyphics weren't always written from left to right, either – they might appear from right to left or downwards. You can tell which way to read by looking at which way the symbols face.

ZOOM IN

The symbols representing names of gods, goddesses and royal people were put in an oval shape with a line at one end, called a cartouche.

Joined-up writing

Hieroglyphics weren't the only form of writing the Ancient Egyptians used. Religious texts were often recorded in a type of joined-up writing called hieratic, which means 'priestly writing'. Instead of being carved in stone, hieratic was written in ink on papyrus, so it was much quicker to write.

Name that...

HIEROGLYPH

Can you understand Egyptian hieroglyphics? Use this guide to hieroglyphics, and then see if you can decode the words on page 51. Then, check your answers on page 88!

Decode these words using the guide
to hieroglyphics on page 50.

1

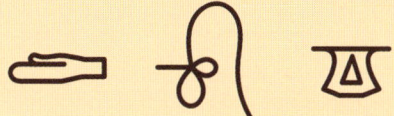

2

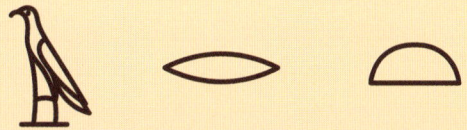

3

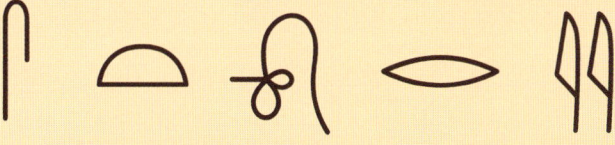

4

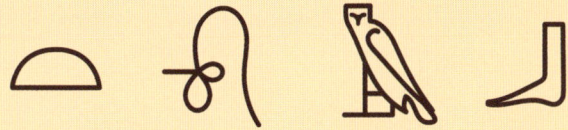

5

SYMBOLS OF EGYPT

The culture of Ancient Egypt was filled with symbols. These represented the most important religious and spiritual ideas. Most people couldn't read or write, but everyone who saw these symbols understood what they meant.

Ankh

The ankh was a cross that was looped at the top so it looked a bit like a key. This symbol represented life and immortality. Gods and goddesses were often pictured holding an ankh to show their power over life and death.

Djed

The djed was shaped like a pillar with four lines across it. It was a symbol of stability and was said to represent the spine of the god Osiris, embodying his triumph over death and his rebirth.

Was sceptre

sceptre

The was sceptre was shaped like a sceptre (a ceremonial staff held by a king or queen), and topped with the head of a dog or fox. It represented power and authority, and its style and colour changed depending on which god or goddess was shown holding it. For example, the was sceptre of the sun god Ra often had a snake attached to it.

The eye of Horus

The eye of Horus was believed to be a powerful symbol that could protect people from evil and give them strength. It stood for sacrifice, healing and restoration.

Scarab

Scarabs are a type of dung beetle. Ancient Egyptians saw them lay their eggs in a ball of dung, which was food for the baby beetles when they hatched. The new beetles then emerged from the dung. Because of this, the scarab represented the idea of eternal life and rebirth, and was an important protective symbol.

FASCINATING FACT

The shen ring was a round shape like a loop of rope. The cartouche shape in hieroglyphics (see page 49) is an elongated version of this symbol of protection and eternity.

Ka

The ka – a person's life force – was often represented by two arms raised up to the sky. This was an important symbol in the art found in tombs because it represented a vital part of a person that needed to carry on existing in the afterlife.

EGYPTIAN ART

The art of Ancient Egypt tells us as much as the writing does about the life, culture and beliefs of this great civilisation. Art and crafts show how important spiritual matters and the natural world were to the Egyptians.

Pottery

Pottery was very important because it was not only beautiful, but useful, too! Items such as pots, urns, jugs and jars were used to store food, water and offerings to the gods. They were often decorated with human scenes or geometric patterns. A type of ceramic called faience was especially highly prized. People believed these shimmering blue-green objects had magical powers.

Faience

Jewellery

The Egyptians were skilled at jewellery-making. They used gold and semi-precious stones such as lapis lazuli to craft beautiful necklaces, bracelets and brooches. These often incorporated amulets – special charms that people believed protected them from disease, evil and bad luck.

Carvings

Important buildings and structures were usually made from stone such as limestone or sandstone, so carvings called reliefs were a common art form. The artwork might be carved into the stone (sunken), or raised, so that it stood out above the surface. Artists carved out these images using copper or bronze tools.

Example of a raised relief carving

Wall paintings

Artists covered the walls of tombs and temples with scenes that could help dead people in the afterlife, or that celebrated the pharaoh or the gods and goddesses. There were pictures of religious rituals and people interacting with the gods and goddesses, as well as farming scenes and other depictions of daily life.

ZOOM IN

Different colours, or pigments, were made out of minerals dug up from the earth. Ochre is a kind of clay that was used for both yellow and red.

PART TWO

See how much you remember about Egyptian religion, beliefs, buildings and culture by answering these questions. Test yourself on everything from gods to temples to ancient art... Good luck!

Check your answers on p.89!

1

Who was the Egyptian god of the sky?

A. Horus

B. Ra

C. Seth

2

Which goddess could become a cat?

A. Isis

B. Bastet

C. Nut

3

What did Anubis weigh a person's heart against to see if they could enter the afterlife?

A. A scarab beetle

B. A reed

C. A feather

4

Which organ was left inside the body during mummification?

A. The brain

B. The lungs

C. The heart

TRUE OR FALSE?

The shape of a pyramid represented a pharaoh's crown.

Find out on p.88!

5 Which Pharaoh was the Great Pyramid at Giza built for?

A. Rameses II

B. Khufu

C. Seti I

6 In a temple, what was the pylon?

A. The gateway to the temple

B. The room where a statue of the temple god or goddess was kept

C. The great hall with giant columns

7 What is a sphinx?

A. A creature with the body of a human and the head of a jackal

B. A creature with the body of a falcon and the head of a human

C. A creature with the body of a lion and the head of a human

8 What material was the pyramid (pyramidion) of an obelisk often covered in?

A. Limestone

B. Electrum

C. Copper

9 What does the word 'hieroglyphics' mean?

A. God's words

B. Sacred carving

C. Picture stories

10 What was the ankh a symbol of?

A. Life

B. Power

C. Stability

57

FARMING

The whole Ancient Egyptian civilisation was founded on farming. Without the fertile soil that the Nile floods created, Egypt would never have grown into a wealthy, successful empire.

Farming seasons

There were three seasons in the Egyptian farming year:

- Akhet was the 'Season of the Inundation', when heavy summer rains caused the Nile to flood. Farmland would disappear under the high waters.
- Peret was the 'Season of the Emergence', when the floodwaters went down, leaving the land covered in a rich, black soil.
- Shemu was the 'Season of the Harvest', when the Egyptian people gathered in their crops to make food and stored seeds to plant the following year.

FASCINATING FACT

The people of Ancient Egypt called their country Kemet, which means 'Black Land' – named after the dark earth left behind from the Nile flood.

Key crops

After the inundation, farmers planted grain – the most important crop in Ancient Egypt. This was used to make bread and beer, and was also a valuable product for trade. Farmers also grew barley, vegetables and fruit such as figs and melons. Another key crop was flax, which was made into a cloth called linen.

A farmer's tools

Egyptian farmers used a sickle for cutting down crops such as wheat and barley. It had a curved blade made of flint (a hard rock) attached to a wooden handle. Farmers also used tools such as a rake to help them gather harvested grain into piles.

Behind the plough

At first, Egyptian farmers used hand ploughs to help them break up the soil ready to plant crops. It was hard work turning the soil by hand, and because the ploughs had to be small and light enough to carry, it took a long time. Later, the Egyptians designed a bigger plough that could be pulled by oxen. The farmers themselves walked behind the plough, breaking up any chunks of soil the plough missed with tools such as a hoe (a tool with a handle and a leaf-shaped wooden blade).

MEDICINE

The Ancient Egyptians got ill and had accidents, just like we do today, so being a doctor was an important job. They took a surprisingly scientific approach to understanding the human body – although their ideas included a dose of magic too!

Exploring the body

One of the main reasons that the Egyptians were good at medicine was because they knew what was inside the body. Thanks to the process of mummification, they learned about organs such as the heart, liver and lungs. Egyptian doctors didn't get everything right, but they were among the earliest people to think in a logical, scientific way about what role the organs played in the body.

It is thought that this wall painting may be showing people having an early form of reflexology (a health treatment that involves applying different amounts of pressure to the feet and hands).

Natural remedies

Egyptian doctors turned to nature and natural remedies for many treatments. They made medicines from lots of different plants and herbs, often mixed with wine. They also realised that putting honey on a wound could cure an infection, and that mouldy bread could do the same. We still make use of honey's natural antibacterial properties today, and of course antibiotics like penicillin are made from mould!

surgical tools used in Ancient Egypt

The first surgeons

Archaeologists have found lots of different surgical tools used in Ancient Egypt, so we know that they performed operations. They were one of the first civilisations to try and set broken bones so that they would heal properly. They may have delivered babies by what we now call caesarean section, and even carried out brain surgery!

Medicine and magic

Not all medicine was based in science. The Egyptians believed that they could get ill because of the actions of evil spirits or angry gods, so they also believed that magic spells, charms and prayers could cure them. As these were often done alongside more traditional medical treatments, who was to say which one was the cure!

TRUE OR FALSE?

The Ancient Egyptians made artificial limbs out of animal bones.

Find out on p.88!

FOOD & DRINK

Food and drink was an important part of everyday life in Ancient Egypt, but the type of food people ate depended on how wealthy they were.

A simple diet

Most ordinary Egyptians, such as farmers and labourers, had a simple but healthy diet. They ate two meals a day. The morning meal was probably bread. The evening meal would also have included bread, along with vegetables such as onions, leeks and radishes. Richer people had a greater variety of food, including some meat. They also enjoyed sweet cakes made from dates and honey.

Luxury meat

People didn't eat meat every day, but when they did it was often pork or mutton (sheep), and perhaps duck or pigeon. They also sometimes ate more exotic animals! At a banquet, hippo might be on the menu, or perhaps wading birds such as cranes.

This wall painting shows some of the meat that wealthy Ancient Egyptians might have eaten, including duck, beef and geese.

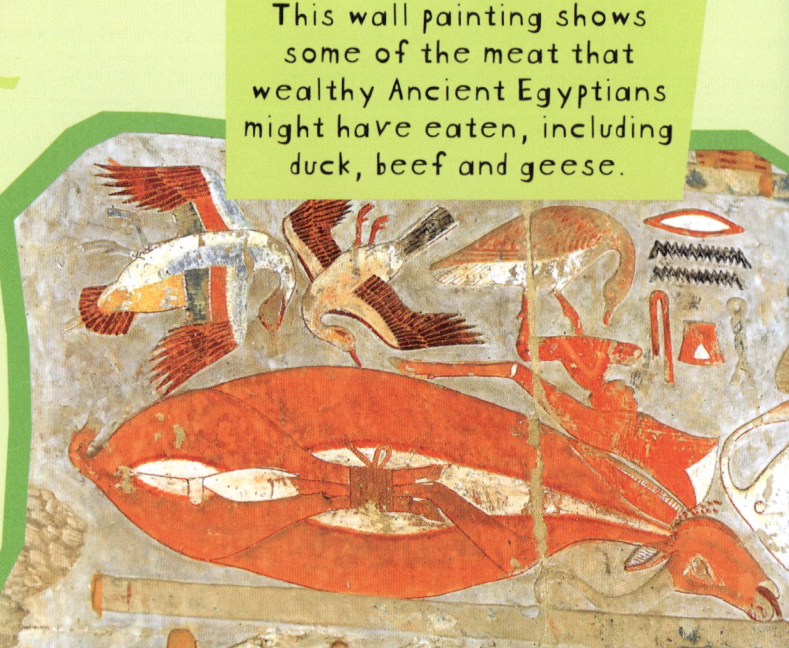

Drink

With the Nile close at hand, you might think the Egyptians had plenty of water to drink. But the river water was dirty, and there was no filtering process. Instead, they drank a type of thick, cloudy beer, with bits floating in it. Beer was made with water, but all the germs were killed in the process of fermentation.

This model from the tomb of an Ancient Egyptian official shows a scene from a bakery and a brewery.

Evidence from art

A lot of what we know about the Ancient Egyptians' diet comes from wall paintings. This is because food played a big part in religion and the afterlife. Tombs were often decorated with pictures of food. Real food was placed inside tombs – and sometimes even fake food made of wood or clay.

TRUE OR FALSE?

The honey found in Ancient Egyptian tombs is still edible.

Find out on p.88!

FASCINATING FACT

The Ancient Egyptians were known to eat hedgehogs! The hedgehog was wrapped in clay and baked over a fire. When it was fully cooked, the clay was cracked open, taking the hedgehog's spikes with it.

A scene showing beekeeping. Ancient Egyptians used honey in cooking and medicines.

LEISURE TIME

The Ancient Egyptians worked hard, but they also knew how to have fun. Thousands of years ago, people enjoyed the same sort of pastimes that we enjoy today!

Sports

The Ancient Egyptians thought that it was important to be physically fit. Children took part in sports from a young age. Boys were taught to swim, wrestle and play a form of hockey. Girls learned to dance and do gymnastics. Sports remained important into adulthood. Wall paintings show people doing all sorts of activities, including boxing, weight-lifting, archery and tug-of-war.

Toys and games

Children played with animals carved out of wood, or dolls and figures of soldiers that were stuffed with grass or hay to give them softer bodies. One of the oldest board games in the world, Senet, was invented in Egypt, and was very popular. Other board games included Hounds and Jackals, and Mehen – the 'Game of the Snake'.

Senet was a popular board game in Ancient Egypt.

Music and dance

As in other ancient civilisations, music and storytelling were very important in Egypt. Storytelling was one way in which the history of the people and their country was shared and passed down the generations. People played instruments such as the harp, flute and drums. Dancers and acrobats would entertain the guests at banquets. At religious festivals, rich and poor alike took part in music and dancing at the celebrations.

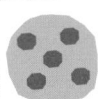

5 popular sports

1. Wrestling: This was an enjoyable sport, particularly for young men, but it was also an important part of military training.

2. Archery: This was both a sport and a vital skill for hunters and soldiers.

3. Swimming: Swimming in the Nile was encouraged from a young age, for fitness and practical reasons.

4. Rowing: Rowing was popular as a competitive sport and as a practical skill for living near the Nile.

5. Stick fighting: This martial-art style sport required balance, strength and control.

stick fighting

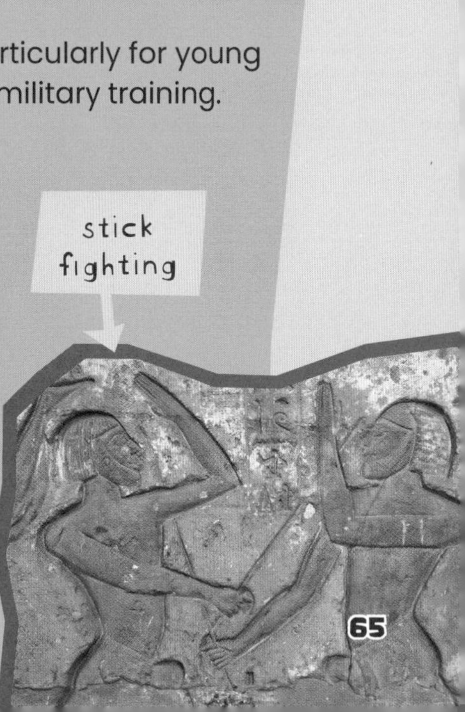

ANCIENT EGYPTIAN LIFE

Get the low-down on what it was like to be an ordinary Ancient Egyptian, with these facts and figures about daily life.

Numbers of the year

In Ancient Egypt, a week was 10 days (called a decan), a month was three weeks (30 days) and a season was four months.

Written remedies

The Ebers Papyrus is one of the earliest known medical texts. The scroll is about 20 metres long and contains more than 800 remedies for everything from stomach ache to bad breath!

Working week

Some experts think that ordinary people worked for eight days of the week, then had two days off – like a weekend – to do leisure activities and worship the gods.

An important village

A village of 68 mud-brick and stone houses, called Deir el-Medina, was discovered near the Valley of the Kings. The tombs, letters and legal documents found there revealed a lot about life in Ancient Egypt.

Counting in hieroglyphs

The Ancient Egyptians used a decimal system, and different symbols to represent numbers. For example, 1 was a single stroke, 100 was a coil of rope and 1,000 was a lotus plant.

Senet statistics

The board game Senet was invented more than 5,000 years ago. The board had a grid of 30 squares in three rows and two sets of pawns of varying numbers (see page 64). However, historians are not entirely sure how Senet was played.

Ancient alphabet

There were more than 700 main hieroglyps in the Ancient Egyptian writing system. A few more than the 26 in the English alphabet!

Jobs for life

Jobs were passed down the generations. Children, particularly from less wealthy families, started learning their family's trade when they were only five years old. They were considered adults at the age of about 14.

Festival culture

The Ancient Egyptians celebrated up to 50 festivals each year. The Opet festival could last for up to 27 days (see page 46)!

There's no place like home

Ordinary people lived in mud-brick houses made up of just two or three rooms. They almost always had flat roofs. Farmhouses might have two levels, with the living quarters on top and a storage area below.

festival procession of soldiers

PAPYRUS

At first, the Ancient Egyptians wrote on pieces of wood or animal skin, or they carved their writing into tablets made of clay or stone. Then, around 2900 BCE, they figured out that they could use a plant called papyrus to make sheets that were much easier to write on.

The papyrus plant

Papyrus is a tall reed-like plant that grew in the marshy areas along the banks of the River Nile in ancient times. The stalk of the plant had a tough green layer on the outside, but inside was a strong, white, fibre-like material that could be cut into strips.

ZOOM IN

The papyrus plant has a triangular stem (and long, sharp leaves).

Making paper

To make a papyrus sheet, the Ancient Egyptians first sliced off the green outer layer, then peeled the white bit inside into thin strips. These were soaked in water, rolled out, then weaved into a sheet in two layers, the upper layer laid crossways over the lower one. The sheet was flattened under a stone slab, then hit with a heavy tool like a hammer to make the fibres in each layer stick together more strongly. The sheet was then dried to make what looked a bit like paper.

The invention of ink

Papyrus sheets were a brilliant invention – but Ancient Egyptians needed something that would write well on this new material. So, they created a type of black ink, made from vegetable gum, beeswax and soot. To make different colours of ink, they replaced the soot with other ingredients, such as ochre to make a red colour.

CALENDARS & CLOCKS

So much of life in Ancient Egypt relied on the Nile floods that it was essential to keep track of the days, months and seasons with accurate calendars and clocks.

The lunar calendar

The Ancient Egyptians had calendars based on both the Sun and the Moon. They initially worked out the dates of religious festivals and other important events based on the phases of the Moon. But they needed a different way to mark out things relating to everyday life, so later they worked out a solar (sun-based) calendar, too.

The solar calendar

The Egyptians noticed that a particular star, Sopdet (the star we call Sirius), appeared in the sky every year at the same time as the Nile flooded. They used this to work out a solar calendar of days and months. Each of the three seasons had four months, each with 30 days in it, making a 360-day year. This wasn't quite long enough, so to stop the months getting out of sync with the seasons, the Egyptians added five extra days at the end of the year, after the third season called Shemu (see page 58). Egyptians didn't have to work on these days, which were used to worship five major gods.

An Ancient Egyptian calendar engraved on a temple wall.

Measuring time

To begin with, the Ancient Egyptians used sundials and hourglasses to measure the time of day. Obelisks also functioned as giant sundials, casting shadows that let people see if it was morning or afternoon, and to note the longest and shortest days of the year.

FASCINATING FACT

At night, time was measured using 'decan stars'. These were groups of stars that rose regularly and were used to split the night into 12 hours.

Water clocks

The invention of the water clock helped the Ancient Egyptians measure time much more accurately. This clever clock was actually a stone bowl with a tiny hole in the bottom. Inside the bowl were evenly spaced marks up the side. The bowl was filled with water, which would drip out at a regular pace. People could tell the time by looking at where the level of water was against the marks.

IRRIGATION METHODS

Farming was vitally important to the Ancient Egyptians, so it's no surprise that some of their most amazing inventions were related to agriculture. In particular, they found some ingenious ways to irrigate their crops (supply the crops with water) in the dry desert landscape.

Reservoirs

Ancient Egyptian farmers had to make the most of the Nile floodwaters when they came. To stop the water disappearing too quickly, they built reservoirs (places to store water) out of mud bricks near their fields. As the floodwater moved back towards the river, some of it got trapped in the reservoirs, where it stayed for farmers to use later.

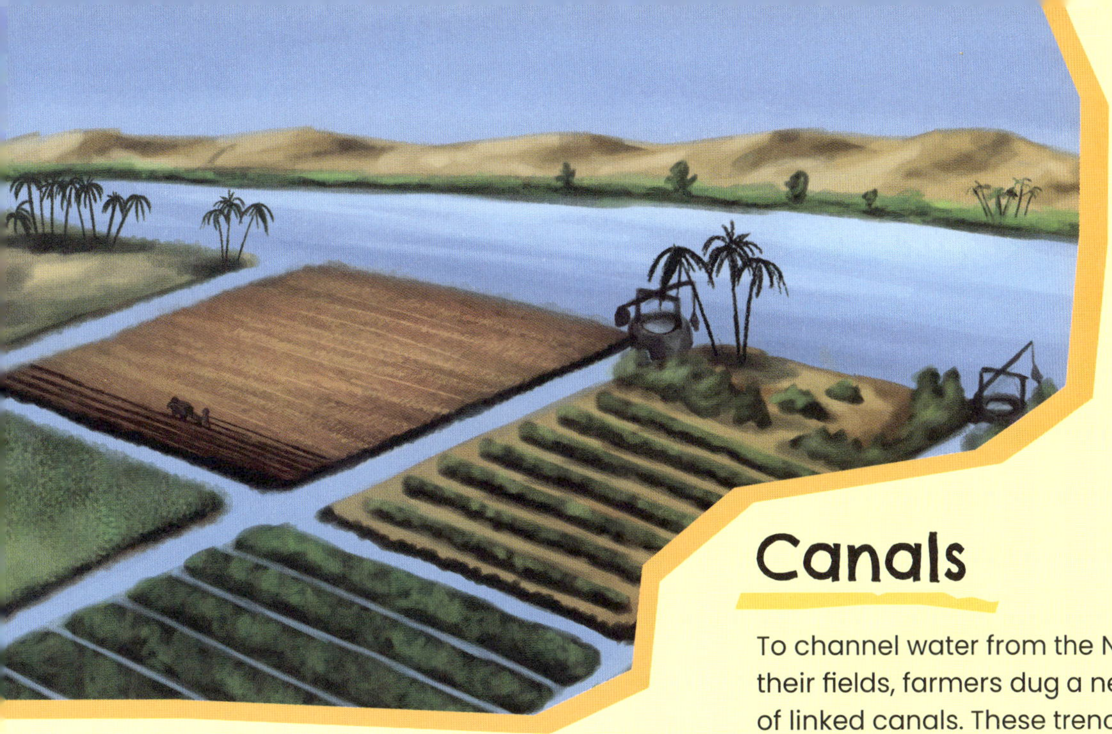

Canals

To channel water from the Nile to their fields, farmers dug a network of linked canals. These trenches allowed them to control the flow of water and to access the river more easily in the dry season. They also acted as storage for water, like small reservoirs.

The shadoof

A shadoof was a simple but clever way of lifting water from a canal. It was made up of a long pole that was balanced on a crossbeam. At one end of the pole was a bucket on a rope and at the other was a heavy counterweight. The farmer lowered the bucket into a canal by pulling on the rope. He raised it, full of water, by pulling down on the counterweight. The pole could then be swung round away from the canal and the water poured onto the crops.

FASCINATING FACT

A nilometer was a device that measured the height of the river water. Nilometers were spaced out along the Nile, so people knew if the river was lower or higher than usual. That way they could be prepared for a period of drought, or for dangerously high floodwaters.

LOOKING GOOD

The Ancient Egyptians cared a lot about personal hygiene and looking good. How well a person dressed, how valuable their jewellery looked, and the kind of make-up they wore all revealed someone's status in society.

Make-up

Eye make-up may have been an Ancient Egyptian invention, and we know from wall paintings that both men and women wore it. Black eye make-up was made from a mineral called galena. Green eye make-up was made from powdered malachite, another mineral. The Egyptians believed that this kind of make-up protected them from the sun's rays, prevented infection and kept away the flies!

FASCINATING FACT

Eye make-up may also have been used to imitate the look of the falcon-headed god, Horus.

Keeping clean

Cleanliness was very important. Wealthy Egyptians might bathe every day, using soap made from a mix of animal fat and ash to wash themselves. They used scented oils to keep their skin soft and smelling nice. Poorer people washed in the Nile.

Queen Hatshepsut

Shaving and beards

The Egyptians can be credited with inventing the razor, which they initially made out of sharp stone blades tied to wooden handles. Most men shaved their facial hair, but they also often wore fake beards. Paintings and statues of pharaohs show them with special ceremonial beards, which indicated their high status. Even Queen Hatshepsut seems to have sometimes worn a beard!

Wigs

Lice were a big problem in Ancient Egypt, so many people shaved their heads to keep the bugs away. Wealthy people didn't go around bald, though – they wore wigs made from human hair. Less wealthy people might wear wigs made from vegetable fibres, horsehair or sheep's wool. The Ancient Egyptians used beeswax and animal fat to make the wigs shiny and keep them in shape.

ANCIENT EGYPT

Meet Aliaa Ismail – an Egyptologist who is exploring the Tomb of Pharaoh Seti I in Egypt. Her mission is to protect the beauty of ancient history and share it with the world.

What kind of things do archaeologists like you do?

There are so many adventures in archaeology! Some people dig and uncover things that have been hidden for thousands of years. Others study, draw, photograph or care for what's already been found, making sure it's safe for the future.

For me, it's important to not only protect objects but also feelings, stories and ways of life. What I love about archaeology is that every day brings a new mystery to discover or a new piece of the story to care for.

How do you explore ancient tombs without even touching them?

In the Valley of the Kings in Egypt, the tombs are thousands of years old, and every tiny crack or flake of colour matters. Touching them, even gently, can cause damage. So instead, we use light! With special tools like laser scanners and high-resolution cameras, we can record every detail... without laying a single finger on the walls. The computer collects all that information and builds a perfect 3D copy we can explore, measure and share.

This way, the tomb stays safe, and people all over the world, even children who've never been to Egypt, can walk through it on a screen and see what it's really like.

What does it feel like to walk inside an ancient tomb?

When you first step into a tomb like the one built for Pharaoh Seti I, it feels as if you're walking straight into history. The air is cool and still, and the walls seem to glow with stories painted thousands of years ago. Every sound, even your own footsteps, feels loud.

We explore tombs carefully and respectfully. We don't go in with hammers or chisels, we go in with cameras, scanners and care. We move slowly, almost like tiptoeing through time. Each scan, each photograph, is a promise to the people who built these places that we'll protect their stories, not take them away.

ARCHAEOLOGY & EGYPTOLOGY

Archaeology is the study of things from civilisations and people in the past. Archaeologists find a site where people lived hundreds or even thousands of years ago, and then dig carefully to find things that have been left behind.

The birth of Egyptology

Life in Ancient Egypt slowly changed. Due to factors such as invasion, famine and internal conflicts, people stopped worshipping the same gods and goddesses, and the temples fell into disuse. Cities were abandoned and tombs were lost in the sands. In 1798, when the French general Napoleon Bonaparte invaded Egypt, he was fascinated by what he saw. People all over the world became interested, and a whole new field of study was born – Egyptology.

Major moments

1799
The Rosetta Stone is found in northern Egypt.

1881
More than 50 mummies of Egyptian royalty, including Rameses II, are found in Deir el-Bahari. They had been hidden by priests to protect them from tomb robbers.

1863
A French archaeologist clears and starts rebuilding the Temple of Seti I at Abydos.

1912
A life-size painted bust of Queen Nefertiti (a sculpture of the upper part of her body) is discovered, and becomes one of the most famous artefacts from Ancient Egypt.

Why has so much survived?

Luckily for us, a lot of buildings and artefacts from Ancient Egypt have survived. This is partly because, unlike a lot of other ancient civilisations, who built using mud and clay, the Ancient Egyptians used stone. This takes a long time to wear away. The dry climate in Egypt also meant that more fragile things like papyrus scrolls and even mummified bodies, which would have decayed in other places, were preserved.

Space archaeology

Some of Ancient Egypt's 'lost' cities and structures have been found thanks to space archaeology. This unusual science uses satellite and infrared imagery to detect tiny changes in the soil and plant life that suggests there may be secrets hidden beneath the sand. Space archaeology allows experts to find streets, temples and even whole cities without searching huge areas on the ground.

1964
The huge temples of Abu Simbel are taken apart and reassembled in a different place, to stop them being destroyed by rising waters, caused by a new dam.

tombs of the pyramid builders

1922
Howard Carter and his team discover Tutankhamun's tomb.

1954
A full-size wooden ship, designed to carry Pharaoh Khufu to the afterlife, is found in the sand by his Great Pyramid.

1990S TO PRESENT DAY
The discovery of a village and tombs of the pyramid builders in Giza proves that pyramid builders weren't slaves, but valued workers.

KING TUT'S TOMB

In 1922, an incredible archaeological discovery stunned the world – an untouched tomb in the Valley of the Kings. When the lead archaeologist peered into the tomb, someone asked if he could see anything. He replied, 'Yes... Wonderful things!'

The forgotten tomb

By the early twentieth century, most people thought that all the tombs that remained in the Valley of the Kings had been discovered. But British archaeologist Howard Carter was sure there was at least one more, hidden beneath the sands. With the support of his financial backer, Lord Carnarvon, he and his team began digging. After years of searching, they discovered a set of stone steps leading underground.

مقبرة توت عنخ آمون

TOMB OF TUT ANKH AMON NO. 62.

The secrets behind the seal

The outer door at the bottom of the steps was sealed up. However, the tomb had been broken into twice, probably shortly after the original burial. Carter and his team discovered that this was the tomb of Tutankhamun, a pharaoh who had died when he was only about 19 years old. He had been buried with more than 5,000 artefacts that had lain quietly in the darkness for more than 3,000 years. The pharaoh's face was covered in a magnificent death mask made of gold and lapis lazuli.

The curse of King Tut

Soon after the discovery of the tomb, bad things started happening to the archaeological team. Carter's pet canary was killed by a cobra. Then three members of the team died in unusual circumstances, including Lord Carnarvon. People began to say that the tomb had been protected by a curse that would punish anyone who entered. Of course, it wasn't true, but the idea of the 'mummy's curse' captured people's imagination.

FAMOUS FIGURE

Howard Carter

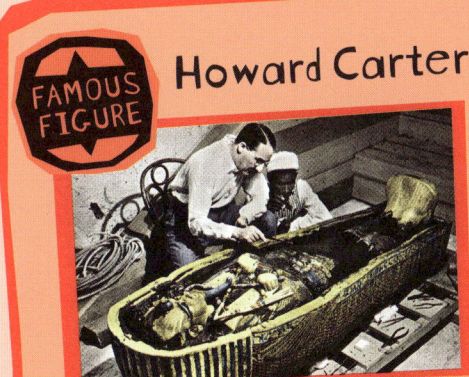

Howard Carter began his career as an artist working on big archaeological sites in Egypt. He became known for his detailed work and the careful records he kept. He felt sure there was an undiscovered tomb in the Valley of the Kings because he had seen lots of artefacts with Tutankhamun's name on. He is now best known for discovering King Tut's tomb.

THE ROSETTA STONE

For hundreds of years after archaeologists discovered hieroglyphics, they couldn't understand them – the mysteries of Ancient Egypt remained a secret in plain sight. Then, an amazing find proved the key to solving this puzzle.

Secrets on a stone

In 1799, some French soldiers stumbled across a large piece of stone in the city of Rosetta in northern Egypt. This dark rock was a piece of an ancient stele – a stone slab decorated with inscriptions or figures – with three pieces of text on it. These were written in three languages: hieroglyphics, a later type of Egyptian writing called Demotic, and Ancient Greek. Scholars realised that this was an important archaeological find to interpret hierogylphs.

The race to translate

Experts knew how to read Ancient Greek, but hieroglyphics were still a mystery. Everyone wanted to crack the code, but even with the helpful Rosetta, no one could figure it out. In 1822, a French scholar called Jean-François Champollion had a breakthrough. He realised that hieroglyphs weren't just pictures of objects – they also represented sounds. Using the Greek text as a guide, he worked out what a lot of the symbols meant. This discovery changed everything. At last archaeologists could start to decipher and read Ancient Egyptian writings on tomb walls, statues and scrolls.

Young's discovery

The text on the Rosetta Stone is a decree honouring the pharaoh Ptolemy V. British scholar Thomas Young noticed that there were six identical signs on the stone – an oval containing the same hieroglyphs. He realised that this was Ptolemy's name, finally proving beyond doubt that royal names were circled with cartouches (see page 49).

FASCINATING FACT

Although experts have worked out what most hieroglyphs mean, there are still some they are not sure about.

Name that...

ARTEFACT

Can you tell a sundial from a sarcophagus? See how many of these ancient objects you recognise, then check your answers on page 88!

1

2

3

4

5

6

7

8

9

10

11

PART THREE

What can you remember about farming, medicine and looking good in Ancient Egypt? Answer the questions on these things and more – good luck!

Check your answers on p.89!

1 Which season was Shemu?

A. The Season of the Inundation

B. The Season of the Emergence

C. The Season of the Harvest

2 What did Egyptians use to treat infections?

A. Honey

B. Papyrus

C. Human hair

3 Which of the following is not an Ancient Egyptian board game?

A. Hounds and Jackals

B. Cat and Mouse

C. The Game of the Snake

4 What was the key ingredient in black ink?

A. Flint

B. Soot

C. Sand

TRUE OR FALSE?

Ancient Egyptians invented one of the first versions of toothpaste.

Find out on p.88!

5 How many months were there in each season in Ancient Egypt?

A. Two

B. Three

C. Four

6 What did a shadoof do?

A. Lift water out of a canal

B. Fix broken bones

C. Flatten papyrus into sheets

7 What colour eye make-up did Ancient Egyptians wear?

A. Red and white

B. Yellow and blue

C. Black and green

8 What is the study of Ancient Egypt called?

A. Egyptology

B. Pyramidology

C. Hierology

9 Which pharaoh's tomb did Howard Carter and his team discover?

A. Tuthmose III

B. Hatshepsut

C. Tutankhamun

10 Which of these languages was not on the Rosetta Stone?

A. Latin

B. Greek

C. Demotic

ANSWERS

True or false?

p.13: TRUE. Not many people in Ancient Egypt had access to the kind of education needed to be able to read and write.

p.23: TRUE. Cleopatra and Julius Caesar had a son together, who was called Caesarion.

p.29: FALSE. Rameses II's reign was one of the longest – 66 years.

p.33: TRUE. Egyptians stayed in mourning for their cat until their eyebrows grew back.

p.34: TRUE. It was thought that this ceremony allowed the dead person to see, speak, hear and breathe, and to receive food and drink, so they could live in the afterlife.

p.57: FALSE. The shape of a pyramid represented the sun's rays.

p.61: FALSE. The Ancient Egyptians didn't make artificial limbs out of animal bones, but they may have made them out of wood and leather.

p.63: TRUE. Honey's unique properties mean that even after all this time, it's still edible today!

p.87: TRUE. The Ancient Egyptians used a paste made of oxen hooves, myrrh, eggshells, pumice and water to remove plaque from their teeth.

Name that...

pp.50–51: Name that... hieroglyph

1. dog
2. art
3. story
4. tomb
5. sport

pp.84–85: Name that... artefact

1. Mirror
2. Razor
3. Hoe
4. Wall painting
5. Senet board
6. Sundial
7. Water clock
8. Sarcophagus
9. Canopic jar
10. Scarab amulet
11. Stele

Quiz yourself on...

pp.28-29: Quiz yourself on...
Part one

1. B. 300,000 years ago
2. A. Lower Egypt and Upper Egypt were united
3. B. Three
4. C. They were farmers.
5. A. Thebes
6. C. A lighthouse
7. B. An administrative region
8. A. 'Great House'
9. C. Cleopatra
10. B. Vizier

pp.56-57: Quiz yourself on...
Part two

1. A. Horus
2. B. Bastet
3. C. A feather
4. C. The heart
5. B. Khufu
6. A. The gateway to the temple
7. C. A creature with the body of a lion and the head of a human
8. B. Electrum
9. B. Sacred carving
10. A. Life

pp.86-87: Quiz yourself on...
Part three

1. C. The Season of the Harvest
2. A. Honey
3. B. Cat and Mouse
4. B. Soot
5. C. Four
6. A. Lift water out of a canal
7. C. Black and green
8. A. Egyptology
9. C. Tutankhamun
10. A. Latin

GLOSSARY

abstract describing things that are ideas or feelings rather than objects you can touch or see

artefact something made and used by people a long time ago, such as pottery, tools or jewellery

chariot a two-wheeled vehicle pulled by horses

counterweight a weight that is designed to balance another weight, making it easier to lift or move heavy things

decay to break down or rot away over a period of time

decimal system a number system based on 10 and that uses ten digits to represent numbers (0 to 9)

decipher to work out what something means when it is particularly difficult or written in code

decree a rule or order given by someone important such as a ruler or judge

deity a god or goddess that people worship

divine describing things that are related to a god or gods

electrum a precious metal made from a mixture of gold and silver, which was used to make jewellery and to cover monuments in ancient times

famine a situation where a lot of people do not have enough food to keep them healthy

fertile land beside the Nile

fertile describing something that is good for growing things in, such as soil that crops grow well in

flax a plant with a long, woody stem that contains fibres used to make the cloth linen

flint a hard dark grey or black rock that ancient people often used to make tools

hierarchy a kind of ranking system where things are organised in order of power or importance

hoe a tool with a thin, flat blade at the end of a long handle

immortality living forever

incense a special substance that smells nice when it burns

inscription a message that is written on or carved into something like stone

inundation when something is completely covered by water

irrigate to bring water to farmland in order to grow crops

jackal a wild animal in the dog family, related to the wolf

lapis lazuli a type of mineral gemstone that has a bright blue colour

lice tiny insects that can live on people's head and crawl around in their hair

necropolis

limestone a type of soft rock often used in building

monument a structure such as a building or statue that is built to commemorate a person or event

myth a traditional story usually created to explain strange things about the world

necropolis a burial place, often a large cemetery within a city

papyrus a tall, reed-like plant that grows along the river Nile

pictogram a picture or symbol that is used to represent data or information

pigment a substance that gives things their colour

a stele

prosperity the state of being successful and having plenty of money

pylon the gateway to an Ancient Egyptian temple, made from two large pillars with a doorway in-between

quarry large, deep pit that stone or minerals are dug out of

ramp a sloping surface that joins two different levels in a structure

reservoir a large, artificial lake that is used to store water to use in dry periods

resurrection coming back to life after dying

ritual a religious ceremony consisting of a series of actions that are carried out in a particular order

sacred describing things that are holy or connected to god or the gods in some way

sceptre a decorated stick or staff carried by royalty during certain ceremonies

scholar someone who studies a particular subject in great detail

scribe a person whose job is to copy out documents, often by hand

scroll a roll of paper or parchment for writing on

shrine a holy place that is dedicated to remembering or worshipping a particular person who has died or a particular holy person or god

stele a tall piece of stone with writing carved into it, often a type of gravestone

syllable a unit of speech that contains a single vowel sound, which forms part of a word

treasury the money that is owned and held by a country, state or kingdom

underworld a mythical place where some cultures believe the dead go, said to be beneath the earth

the Sphinx

INDEX